THE WORLD HERITAGE

GREAT ANIMAL REFUGES

CHICAGO

Table of Contents

Introduction 4
Isolated Refuges 10
Timeline 14
Life on an Archipelago 16
Passports? Gnus Need Not Apply 18
The Rain Forest 20
Special Terms 22
The Savannah 26
Glossary 32
Index 33

Library of Congress Cataloging-in-Publication Data
Serra Naranjo, Rafael.
 [Grandes refugios de fauna. English]
 Great animal refuges / by Rafael Serra Naranjo.
  p. cm. — (The World heritage)
  Translation of: Grandes refugios de fauna.
  Includes index.
   Summary: Discusses wildlife refuges in various parts of the world and their importance in preserving animals in their natural habitats.
   ISBN 0-516-08385-6
 1. Wildlife refuges—Juvenile literature. 2. National parks and reserves—Juvenile literature. 3. Natural history—Juvenile literature. [1. Wildlife refuges. 2. Wildlife conservation.] I. Title. II. Series.
QL83.S4713 1993
639.9'5—dc20   93-3437
                                                                     CIP
                                                                      AC

Grandes refugios de fauna: © INCAFO S.A./Ediciones S.M./UNESCO 1988
Great Animal Refuges: © Childrens Press,® Inc./UNESCO 1993

ISBN (UNESCO) 92-3-102588-0
ISBN (Childrens Press) 0-516-08385-6

Great Animal Refuges

Living things inhabit every corner of our planet, from ocean depths to mountaintops. Plants and animals have even colonized places that seem quite inhospitable to life. Deserts and polar regions, for instance, shelter flora and fauna perfectly adapted to their harsh conditions.

The part of the atmosphere where life can develop is known as the biosphere. The biosphere extends from the earth's surface up to the ozone layer. Carried by the wind, myriads of tiny insects, arachnids, and plants ascend to a height of 2.5 miles (4 kilometers). A vertebrate, the Andean condor, can fly at an altitude of 4.3 miles (7 kilometers). As high as 6.8 miles (11 kilometers), some bacteria and fungus spores can be found.

Organisms are so determined to use every available ecological niche that they even dwell in ocean caverns 30,000 feet (9,000 meters) deep. Some anaerobic bacteria survive in petroleum deposits 13,000 feet (4,000 meters) below the earth's surface, isolated from any other form of life.

In Search of Water
The climate of the savannah varies with the seasons. Periods of rain and abundance alternate with times of scarcity. Wild animals depend completely on the fluctuating water supply. As the water-holes disappear during the dry season, animals gather in places where a little water can still be found. At these times it is not unusual to find lions drinking near the meadows where zebras graze.

Only a very few types of places on earth are completely devoid of any hint of life. These places include the inner part of volcanoes, some regions that are covered with ice, the depths of certain lakes and parts of the ocean, and very acidic soils.

After thousands of years of evolution, living things have adjusted to unique conditions in every region of the globe. Where there is a warm climate and plenty of moisture, there is a rich and varied array of life forms. In other places, where a harsh climate and poor environment hamper the development of lush vegetation, only a small living community has sprung up. Yet even this small ecosystem is as balanced as those in more favorable regions.

Living things are compelled to expand and diversify, to take over every possible niche. This sweeping process is limited only by the capacity of each biogeographical region to sustain a specific community.

Population Control
While adult elephants lack natural enemies, zebras are subject to attack by the savannah's predators. In this way lions, hyenas, and other predators help to control the zebra population. In the case of the elephant, accidents to the young and environmental limitations determine the number of individuals.

Lying in Ambush
The cheetah, an African member of the cat family, is the fastest land animal in existence. It can accelerate from zero to 45 miles an hour (72 kilometers an hour) in 2.5 seconds! It can reach a speed of 60 miles (100 kilometers) per hour. However, it can only maintain this speed for a few seconds. The cheetah must calculate its attack very carefully so that its energy is rewarded.

For Mutual Benefit
Various species of herbivores often gather together in large groups. This habit has advantages for all the members of the herd, as each species has particular strengths in recognizing danger. Giraffes can survey their surroundings from an elevated position, as can ostriches. Giraffes view the world from 8 feet (2.5 meters) above the ground, and they are known to keep watch while other animals graze. Impalas and other small antelopes serve the community with their hearing and their sense of smell. Each grazing herbivore must help the rest of the herd. The animals take turns feeding, for their powers of observation are limited when their heads are down.

The hartebeest is a bit of an exception. It has an elongated face with eyes set far back on its head. It can graze and somewhat keep watch at the same time. Still, the hartebeest herd has its sentries, too.

Isolated Regions

Every living thing has an effect—makes a difference—in its community. It is a vital part of the natural balance among the plants and animals around it. Nevertheless, most species cannot do anything to make up for the shortcomings of their own physical structures. Nor can they change their environment in any significant way. Human beings are the only creatures capable of extending their influence over the entire planet.

The history of life on earth is the story of a dynamic process. The human species has brought about such rapid changes that natural processes have been unable to absorb them.

A few primitive cultures blend perfectly into the natural environment around them. But advanced civilizations have multiplied so quickly that they have established a new, but unstable, balance. The human species has been so successful that it has overcome biogeographical boundaries and settled almost every region of the earth.

As human civilization advances, plant and animal communities recede. Regions where humans have lived the longest have suffered the deepest changes.

For centuries, European soil has produced crops, pastures, timber, and mineral products. The continental shelf—the waters along the edges of continents—has been over-exploited for fishing. Like the land, even the air shows the effects of a dense population and a super-industrialized civilization.

On the other hand, there are regions that are hard to reach or that have harsh conditions. These areas have escaped large human populations and remain in harmony with natural events.

At one time, it seemed that some of the most remote spots on earth were doomed to invasion by human civilization. Yet today people are more aware of the importance of these untouched environments. Each of these places is a great storehouse of natural resources. Each is also a refuge for many species that cannot be found anywhere else on earth. In addition, these areas are enlightening examples of natural organization.

Perhaps by studying these places, we can find answers to the many questions that still baffle scientists.

The areas of most interest to scientists are those that are geographically isolated. They include nature reserves that are maintained in industrialized countries, well removed from big cities or exploited regions.

Water and Mud
The presence of a watercourse transforms the landscape. Formations that botanists call "gallery forests" are common in Africa. They are forests growing along rivers that flow through essentially arid regions. These narrow forest strips shelter animals that could not survive anywhere else. Some African species, such as the Cape buffalo *(opposite page, bottom)*, not only need water to drink. They also wallow in the mud to protect themselves from parasites.

11

In South America, there are many well-preserved natural areas. This is because so much of South America is still in the early stages of modern economic development. Its biological reserves cover wide areas, too.

The only other large natural areas that remain unchanged by humans are in Africa, in certain parts of Asia, and in the tundra areas in extreme northern latitudes.

Africa is a sparsely populated continent, barely known to Europeans until the 1800s. Much of its vast area offers harsh living conditions for humans, and its rather poor soil is not well suited to agriculture.

Furthermore, the land is subject to an uneven climate. Near the equator, where the climate does not vary much, farming is limited to small plots of land. The soil is exhausted quickly and is soon overgrown with natural vegetation. People who live here are forced to lead a nomadic or semi-nomadic existence. This is partly because they cannot cultivate the jungle or the savannah (grasslands) for too long. Other factors are the uneven rainfall the spontaneous fires that sweep the plains.

The large wild animals of Africa are nomadic, too. In their seasonal migrations, herbivores (plant-eaters) seek the best grazing land. Behind them come the carnivores (flesh-eaters), also in search of food.

Human Origins
This hill at the Olduvai Gorge *(right)* in Tanzania shows what profound changes can take place with the passage of time. The original plain is now found at the top of the plateau. The forces of erosion have worn the surrounding land down to its present state. One consequence of this process is that we have discovered in the gorge the fossil remains of the first known hominids, or human-like beings.

Victim of a Dark Legend
Only recently have we discovered that hyenas are often active predators. This still has not changed the hyena's nasty reputation as an eater of carrion, or animals that are already dead. Hyenas do hunt for some of the prey they consume, and they often steal freshly-killed prey from other animals. They never let any good food go to waste.

Timeline

1934 Albert National Park is created, known later as Virunga (Zaire).
1951 The broad savannahs of Serengeti (Tanzania) are declared a national park.
1959 The Galapagos Archipelago in Ecuador is declared a national park.
1979 The Galapagos Archipelago and the Ngorongoro Conservation Zone (Tanzania) are included on UNESCO's World Heritage list.
1980 Virunga National Park is included on the World Heritage list.
1981 Serengeti National Park is included on the World Heritage list.

The Limits of Growth
The abundance or scarcity of some animals is determined by the environment's capacity to sustain their population. Zebras and gnus (also called wildebeests) dominate the African savannahs, thanks to the enormous quantity of available food. The gnu also has a physical resistance to bovine fever. On the other hand, some very specialized birds, such as the martial eagle *(left),* hardly number one individual to every 20 square miles (5,000 hectares).

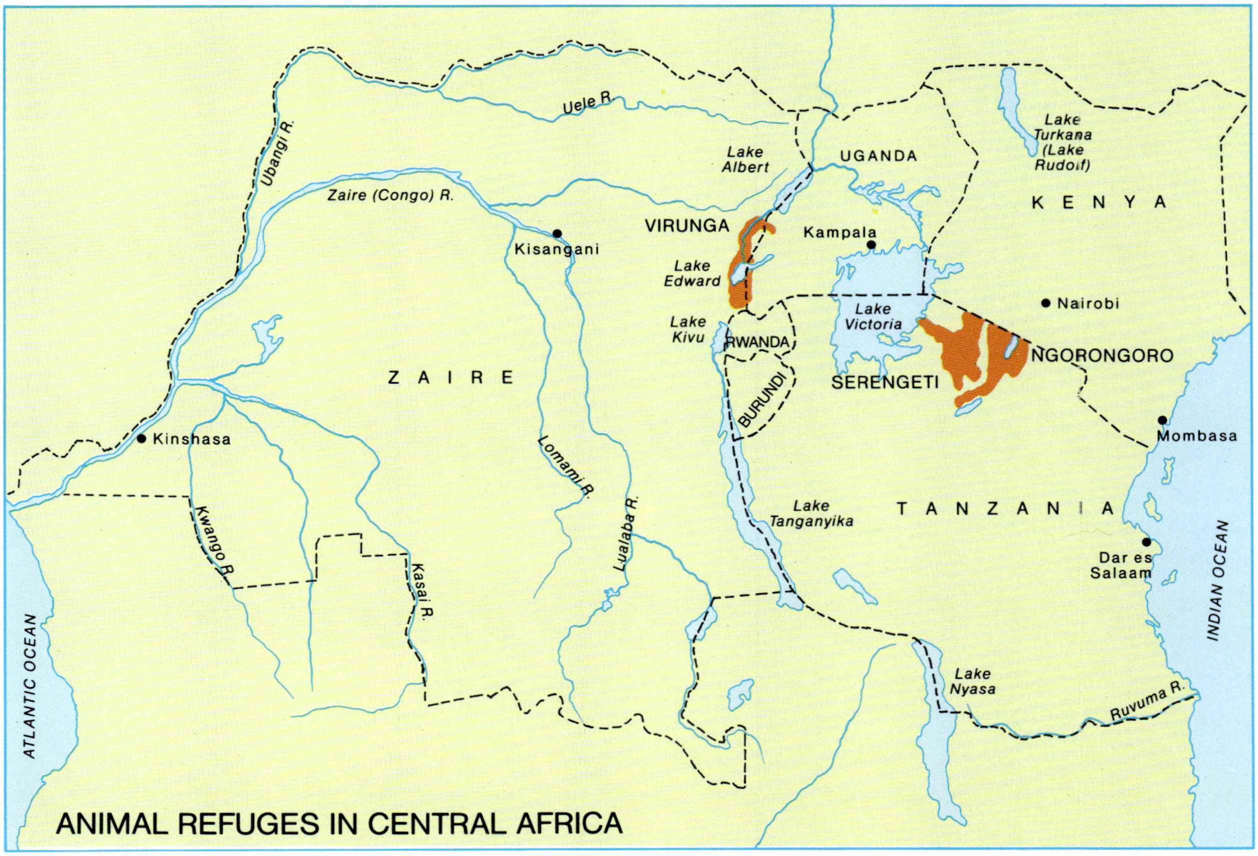
ANIMAL REFUGES IN CENTRAL AFRICA
Uele R.
Ubangi R.
Zaire (Congo) R.
Lake Albert
UGANDA
Lake Turkana (Lake Rudolf)
KENYA
VIRUNGA
Kampala
Kisangani
Lake Edward
Nairobi
Lake Victoria
Lake Kivu
RWANDA
NGORONGORO
ZAIRE
SERENGETI
BURUNDI
Kinshasa
Mombasa
Lomami R.
Kwango R.
Lake Tanganyika
TANZANIA
Lualaba R.
Kasai R.
Dar es Salaam
INDIAN OCEAN
ATLANTIC OCEAN
Lake Nyasa
Ruvuma R.

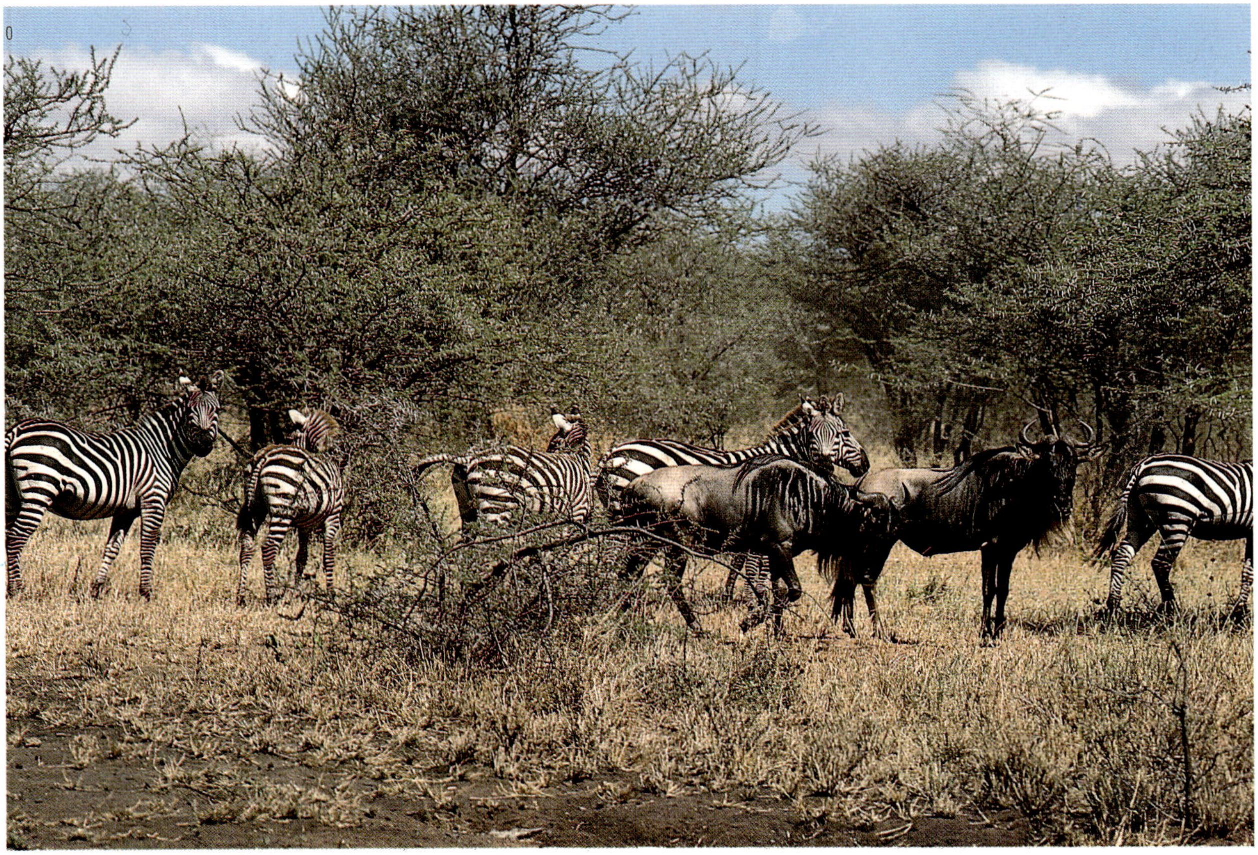

Life on an Archipelago

The ways of life for animals and plants in isolated places change very slowly. Where no people live, these changes are not as abrupt as those that are caused by modern civilization. But this does not mean that life is standing still where there are no outside influences. There are constant changes—they just take place over a long period of time.

One of the most fascinating isolated regions on earth is the Galapagos Archipelago. There the English naturalist Charles Darwin gathered facts that led him to devise his theory of biological evolution

The Colon Archipelago, the official Spanish name for the Galapagos, lies in the Pacific Ocean some 620 miles (1,000 kilometers) off the coast of Ecuador. Politically, the island group is a province of Ecuador.

At no time in their geologic history were these islands part of another land mass. They rose from the sea as a result of intense volcanic activity. Volcanoes still shake this region today, making it one of the earth's "hot spots."

The Galapagos Islands were formed around three million years ago. Once the Galapagos arose, they were a wide-open, untouched territory, ready to be colonized by creatures from the mainland or the sea.

From the time they emerged, the islands have been a refuge for stranded creatures. It is believed that the first arrivals came by chance. Perhaps they arrived aboard rafts of vegetation floating down the rivers on the eastern slope of the Andes Mountains. Pushed by the wind or carried by ocean currents, they eventually reached the Galapagos.

These pioneers found a barren terrain, far from the mainland and almost devoid of things they needed to live. Survival was nearly impossible. Nevertheless, little by little, more new plants and animals arrived and formed colonies of their own.

Gradually, conditions became more favorable for the earlier arrivals. A unique mix of plants and animals developed. Colonies on each separate island adapted to the conditions on that island.

These plant and animal communities developed on their own. Each species became so specialized that it was completely distinct from its ancestors on the mainland. Thus, the inhabitants of the Galapagos are related to South American flora and fauna, but they have evolved into separate, independent species.

A Nest on the Ground
Masked boobies, also called white boobies, always build their nests on the ground—if a simple depression in the earth can be called a nest. There the breeding pair take turns sitting on the solitary egg. While raising the chick, the adults make frequent trips to the sea in search of food. Masked boobies travel to ocean regions far from shore. Thus, they avoid competition with other booby species.

Studying the creatures of the Galapagos helped Darwin form his ideas about how different species develop. His theory of evolution explains the history of life as a dynamic process, subject to constant adjustments. Darwin proposed that, over time, animal and plant species undergo a process called natural selection. That is, in order to survive, they gradually change in response to changing conditions around them.

The effects of natural selection are more obvious in the Galapagos Archipelago than anywhere else on earth. That is why these islands are an invaluable wildlife preserve. No amphibians or freshwater fish live there, but there is an extensive population of reptiles and birds.

Passports?
Gnus Need Not Apply

Several decades ago, gnus were not as numerous as they are today. But the species has fiercely resisted the epidemic of bovine fever, a disease that has decimated African cattle and many species of wild herbivores. The enormous gnu population now places great pressures on the grasslands of East Africa.

During the rainy season, gnus graze at the southern end of Serengeti National Park, beside the Ngorongoro Crater and the Masai Reserve. From there they migrate in search of fresh grazing land, moving slowly toward Lake Victoria. Toward the end of July, they cross the border between Tanzania and Kenya and enter the Masai-Mara Reserve. The return journey follows a more direct course, encircling all of Serengeti. Gnus depend on the grasslands to live. Many carnivores depend in turn on the gnus, and migrate behind them.

From time to time, these immense herds of gnus arrive at a river. The spectacle of thousands of animals fighting to overcome the barrier is unforgettable.

As the enormous herd crosses a river, the gnus crush and drown one another, leaving dead and maimed animals and lost calves behind. These unfortunate ones provide food for carnivores and vultures for weeks.

For wildlife, rivers are far more important boundaries than any political borders drawn by human beings. This is especially true of the gnus. The boundary they cross between Kenya and Tanzania is a straight line on the map—a legacy of a colonial past without regard for physical and cultural realities.

But gnus know nothing of passports, visas, and borders. They only follow their ancient path, year after year.

Mammals in the Galapagos
Every year, the South American sea lion comes to breed on the shores of the Galapagos Islands. The males arrive first and begin their skirmishes over territory. Two weeks later the females arrive, ready to bear the offspring conceived during the previous breeding season. The males try to hold their territory and to gather a harem of females. After the young are born the colonies disperse, although the pups remain with their mothers for about six weeks.

The best-known species is the giant Galapagos turtle, which gave the archipelago its name. Another unique reptile is the marine iguana. It feeds entirely on marine algae. Like all cold-blooded animals, it cannot regulate its own body temperature, so it has to make careful use of the energy it receives from sunlight. When the sun is out it is most active, feeding on its daily ration of algae. In order to feed, it must enter the ocean, whose waters are quite cool due to the Humboldt Current.

Subspecies of turtles, iguanas, and snakes are distributed throughout the archipelago. A single island may have several subspecies.

About 70 percent of the vertebrate animal species on the Galapagos are birds. There are gaudy species, such as the blue-footed booby and the flightless cormorant, as well as gulls, frigate birds, albatrosses, and finches.

There are few native mammals. They include two bat species and a few kinds of rodents, as well as the sea lions that breed on the shores. The other mammals on the islands have been introduced by humans in recent times, dangerously altering the environment's delicate natural balance. The unique ecosystem of the Galapagos is one of the most threatened zones on the planet.

The Rain Forest

In some isolated regions of the South American mainland, the influence of the industrial age has still not been felt. In many cases the isolation is not physical (as in the Galapagos) but geographical, as in the upper basin of the Amazon. The Amazon River is the world's greatest watercourse.

The best preserved region extends from the eastern slope of the Andes to the sources of the Amazon. Brazil, with a total area of over 3 million square miles (8.5 million square kilometers), has only about 770 square miles (200,000 hectares) under cultivation. Nevertheless, this does not mean that the majority of its original forests remain intact. In fact, the great Atlantic forests were destroyed during the colonial era. A great swath of forest is now suffering the same fate because of logging and development.

The rain forest is the result of a stable climate, with consistently high temperatures day and night throughout the year. In addition, it receives more than 80 inches (200 centimeters) of precipitation a year and has a humidity of about 90 percent.

Color Code
Macaws belong to the family Psittacidae, a group of birds found throughout tropical regions of the New and Old Worlds. Their bright plumage serves important purposes in a multi-colored environment such as the Amazon jungle. For instance, the plumage may enable them to attract mates. Or, if the area is sparsely populated with macaws, the bright color may help individuals locate one another and aid group cohesion.

Under these warm, moist conditions, life bursts forth in astonishing diversity. One characteristic of the jungle is the enormous variety of plant and animal species. This does not mean, however, that we find great numbers of creatures within any given species. Although many different species live in the rain forests, there may be only a few examples of some species. There is no section of a rain forest that contains just a few characteristic species. All of the inhabitants flourish, using every available ecological niche.

Manu National Park sprawls over 5,800 square miles (1.5 million hectares) in the rain forests of Peru. It stretches across the districts of Cuzco and Madre de Dios. Depending on geography and climate, only certain types of vegetation are found in any one area on the planet. Within Manu National Park are sixteen different vegetation regions, from the Andean mountainsides to the Amazon plain.

In the rain forests of Manu live the charapas. These aquatic turtles sunbathe in densely packed groups on a riverbank or tree trunk. There are also the terrible piranha, two species of lizard, and the bushmaster. A tropical pit viper, the bushmaster is one of the most dangerous snakes in the world. It is also the largest venomous snake in the Western Hemisphere.

Bird life in Manu is extremely abundant. Aquatic species are most common. Because of periodic rises in the water level of the Amazon River, the ground is marshy nearly everywhere. Some of the park's birds are anhingas, cormorants, herons, spoonbills, and other waterfowl. There are birds of prey in the jungle, too, such as caracaras, vultures, and turkey buzzards. In addition there are brilliantly colored parrots, macaws, and passerines, or perching birds.

King of the Jungle
From an airplane, the Amazon jungle looks like a tapestry of vegetation, enclosed by the curves of a river (in this case, the Manu, *upper right*). The diversity of flora and fauna in this impenetrable environment is unequaled anywhere on the planet. Of all the animals in the rain forests of tropical America, the jaguar *(lower right)* is at the top of the ecological pyramid. It is a super-predator, perfectly adapted to the half-terrestrial, half-aquatic environment of the rain forest.

Special Terms

anaerobe: an organism that does not use free oxygen, but uses some other substance for its metabolism to work properly.

biogeography: a branch of biology concerned with the geographic distribution of animals and plants.

biomass: the estimated mass made up of all the living things in a given area. It is composed of the vegetable biomass and the animal biomass.

biome: a distinct type of ecological community, such as the desert or the savannah.

biosphere: the part of the earth where life can exist, whether on the earth's surface, beneath it, or above it.

An Herbivore's Paradise

The savannah is typical of the central regions of East Africa. It is covered with grasslands and occasional clumps of trees, mostly acacias and baobabs. The nature of the savannah's soil layer determines its plant life. Vegetation that needs deep, fertile soil cannot grow there. But gramineous (grassy) plants can take root in the thin soil. So can trees that spread shallow roots along the surface of the ground. This land supports the greatest herbivore population on the planet.

As for mammals, Manu is home to thirteen of the nineteen primate species that live in Peru's wildlife preserves. These include capuchin monkeys, spider monkeys, and the famous howler monkeys, the largest primates in the neo-tropics. Another mammal of the Amazon jungle is the sloth, a toothless creature that moves in slow motion to avoid being spotted by its many enemies. There are also tapirs and peccaries. And, lying in wait for them all, is the lord of the Amazon, the jaguar.

There are so many different species in the rain forest that it confounds modern science. Scientists suspect that countless species of insects and amphibians have yet to be discovered.

The Savannah

The jungle that grows in the region around the earth's equator was once far more extensive. Twenty-five million years ago, during the Miocene Epoch, the earth's climate was much more humid than it is in our times. The Sahara and Arabian deserts did not exist. Nearly all of Africa was covered by a dense jungle that spread uninterrupted from the Atlantic coast to the shores of the Indian Ocean. Rain forests also extended from India to Southeast Asia. The animal life throughout this entire region was almost identical.

But when the climate changed, the jungle gradually dwindled. As deserts arose, animal species in Africa were separated from those in Asia, and both groups began to evolve separately.

Such natural changes may seem sudden on the geological calendar. But from a human point of view, they are almost unnoticeable. It took thousands of years for the deserts to develop. They are still expanding today, partly due to the overgrazing of cattle.

The savannah is a biome, or ecological community, that exists part way between the desert and the steaming jungle. Deserts receive less than 10 inches (25 centimeters) of rainfall a year and have sparse vegetation. Rain forests receive over 80 inches (200 centimeters) of rainfall a year. But savannahs get 40 to 60 inches (100 to 150 centimeters) a year and have a distinct dry season.

Savannahs include a wide range of ecosystems, making the transition from desert to rain forest in a series of distinct steps. The great African savannahs are the result of a change in climate. This same change made the rain forest recede to its present location along the equatorial belt.

The Heavyweights
Rhinoceroses, hippopotamuses, and elephants are the heaviest land animals on earth. It is no accident that these mountains of flesh, with their strictly vegetarian diet, live on the African savannahs, where the supply of plants and grasses is assured. Hippopotamuses *(right)* are still numerous in some protected African rivers. But the rhinoceros, like this female black rhino with her young *(above)*, survives with difficulty even in protected national parks.

The layer of fertile soil in the savannah is very thin. It rests on a bed of solid lava from volcanoes that once shook this region. Mount Kenya, the Ngorongoro Crater, and the Virunga volcanoes remain as evidence. This soil composition encourages the growth of fields and thickets. Such vegetation does not need deep roots to search for nourishment. Only a few trees have adapted to the dry seasons and thin soil. These include acacias and baobabs.

In Manu National Park, the atmospheric conditions are stable and the diversity of species is enormous, though each species is poorly represented. In contrast, the African savannahs are subject to seasonal changes in climate, with periods of rain and drought. Here there is much less diversity, but the organisms found on the grasslands multiply in tremendous numbers.

The jungle boasts the greatest concentration of plants within a given area. The savannahs can claim the greatest concentrations of animal life on the planet.

The Clean-up Crew
Marabous are members of the stork family, but they have very different feeding habits. They specialize in consuming carrion, or dead animals. Along with vultures and several species of mammals, they are in charge of removing the corpses that appear every day on the savannahs.

A Solitary Male
A solitary lion is either a monarch who has lost his throne, or a vagabond youth who has not yet gathered a harem. The great males regularly survey the boundaries of their territory, marking it to make their magnificent presence known.

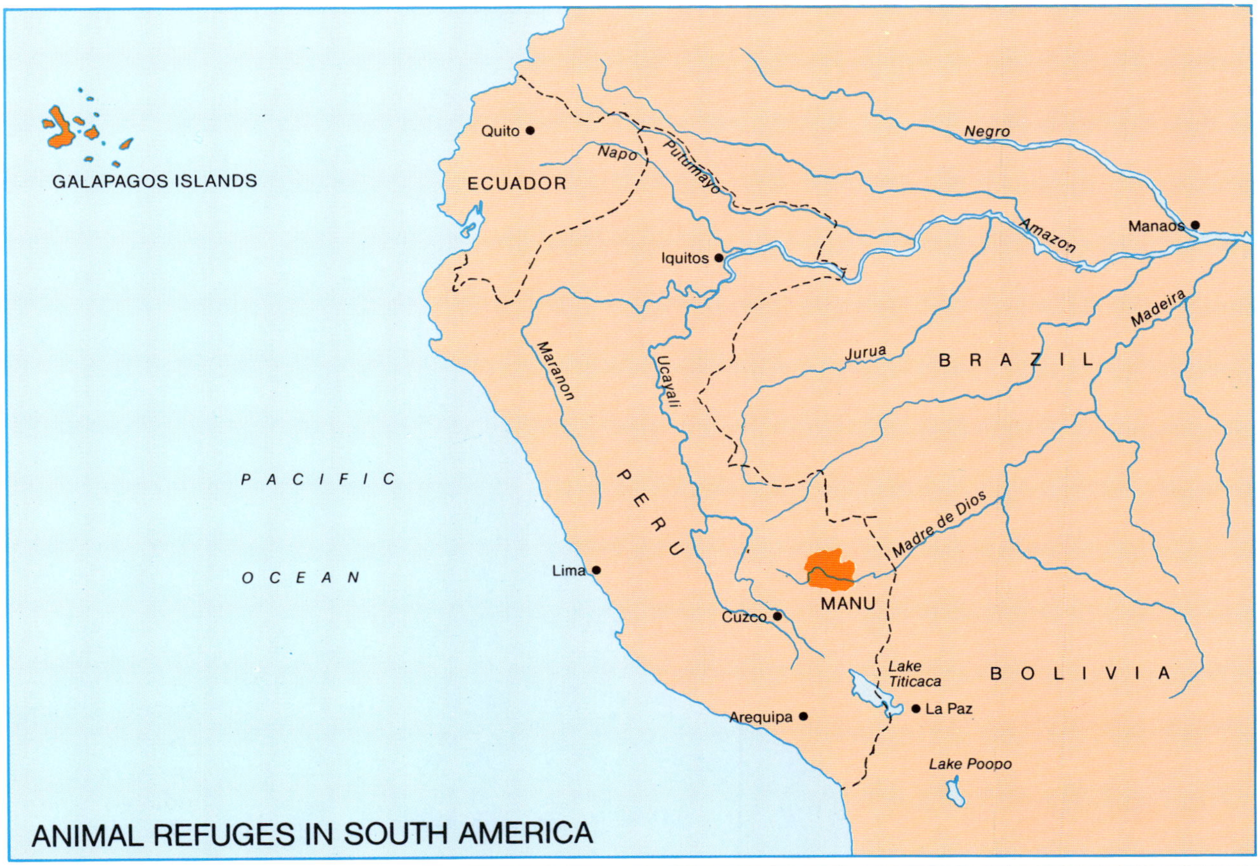

ANIMAL REFUGES IN SOUTH AMERICA

To understand the animal populations of the savannah, look at this visual census of large mammals that was taken in Serengeti National Park (Tanzania) recently. In an area of 5,700 square miles (1.5 million hectares), surveyors counted 1,500,000 gnus, 1 million Grant's and Thompson's gazelles, 200,000 zebras, 76,000 impalas, 74,000 buffaloes, 65,000 topis, 18,000 elands, 9,000 giraffes, 5,000 elephants, 4,000 hyenas, 3,000 lions and 500 cheetahs.

Another example of large animal populations can be seen in the Ngorongoro Crater. This wide volcanic crater joins Serengeti, but is isolated from the rest of the savannah by steep cliffs. Here we find a stable, balanced animal community. As in Serengeti, the herds of plant-eating animals number in the thousands. These animals, in turn, provide an enormous food supply for a large population of predators—hyenas, leopards, cheetahs, and lions.

One of Africa's great wildlife preserves, Virunga National Park in Zaire, contains both the enormous populations of the savannah and the exuberant diversity of the jungle. There are some rare mountain species as well. In this volcanic, mountainous landscape, the biogeographical regions are based on altitude—savannah, rain forest, and mountainside. The park is a mosaic of all the African ecosystems: rain forest, desert, and seacoast. In the moist jungles of Virunga live two of Africa's rarest animals: the okapi and the mountain gorilla.

All of the world's great wildlife preserves have been created for the clear purpose of conservation. They try to prevent any human intrusion that could threaten the survival of these magnificent natural enclaves. Some parks are dangerously overpopulated by animal species, driven there by pressures from unprotected areas outside. Such overpopulation can wear down the environment. The ideal goal is to maintain things as they are, to keep park areas from being reduced, and to harmonize the interests of wildlife with those of the nations that oversee the reserves.

The citizens of these nations are the ones who benefit the most from the immense riches that nature has bestowed on them. For many African countries, wildlife conservation is good business, bringing in important revenues to the public treasury.

There is only one way to save protected areas such as Galapagos, Manu, Serengeti, Ngorongoro, or Virunga. That is to show their guardian nations that they can gain even greater economic, scientific, and cultural benefits by conserving these areas than by destroying them. If these refuges should be lost, we will all suffer the loss.

Under Legal Protection
The hippos of Virunga, the turtles that sun themselves in the Manu River, the various creatures of Bartholomew Island in the Galapagos, and the giraffes of Ngorongoro Crater are all under legal protection. They form part of the legacy that we must preserve and pass on to future generations. But it is useless to protect an isolated species when its natural environment is in danger. National parks around the world attempt to preserve natural areas of exceptional ecological value.

These Sites Are Part of the World Heritage

Galapagos Islands: This archipelago of volcanic origin consists of 13 main islands, 6 lesser islands, and 42 islets. They are home to the Galapagos turtle, the marine iguana, and many other species and subspecies that are found nowhere else on earth.

Manu National Park: The Manu River Basin is the hub of this park, which covers 5,800 square miles (1.5 million hectares) from the Amazon plains to the slopes of the Andes. Flourishing within this area are the majority of all ecosystems possible on the South American continent.

Serengeti National Park: This park spans nearly 5,800 square miles (1.5 million hectares), covered by savannahs and vast grasslands. Today the world's greatest concentration of land animals is found in Serengeti.

Ngorongoro Conservation Zone: This is an immense volcanic crater, from two to three miles (three to five kilometers) in diameter. It is adjacent to Serengeti but is isolated from the rest of the savannahs by steep cliffs with heights of 9,800 to 11,000 feet (3,000 to 3,400 meters).

Virunga National Park: Virunga is considered a showcase of African landscapes. In this enclave one can experience savannahs and flood plains, as well as the impenetrable heights of the Ruwenzori Range, with a wide assortment of equatorial rain forests in between.

Glossary

arachnids: animals belonging to a class that includes spiders, scorpions, mites, and ticks

archipelago: a group of islands

biogeographical region: a type of land region that supports certain kinds of plants and animals

carnivore: a flesh-eating animal

carrion: dead and rotting animal flesh

colonize: to settle in a new location and establish a life there

evolution: a gradual change in the features of plant or animal species as they adjust to changing conditions in their environment

fauna: animals

flora: plants

herbivore: a plant-eating animal

inhospitable: not friendly or supportive

myriads: a great many

neotropics: a biogeographical region that includes South America, tropical parts of North America, and the West Indies

nomadic: leading a life of wandering from place to place

ozone layer: a layer of the atmosphere that is high in ozone, a form of oxygen made of three atoms instead of two; located about 20-30 miles (32-48 kilometers) above the earth's surface

savannah: a grassland in a tropical area, having scattered trees and bushes that resist drought

vertebrate: an animal that has a spinal column

Index

Page numbers in boldface type indicate illustrations.

Africa, 12, 18, 26-30
Amazon River region, 20-22, **23,** 26
Andean condor, 4
Andes Mountains, 16, 20, 22
Asia, 12
biosphere, 4
boobies (birds), **17,** 20
Brazil, 20
bushmasters (snakes), 22
Cape buffalo, **11**
charapas (turtles), 22, **31**
cheetah, **6**
Darwin, Charles, 16, 18
deserts, 26
eagle, martial, **14**
Ecuador, 16-20
elephants, **7,** 26
evolution, theory of, 18
Galapagos Archipelago, 16-20, **19,** 30, 31, **31**
gallery forests, 10
giraffes, **8-9, 31**
gnus, 14, **15,** 18
gorillas, 30
hartebeests, 8
hippopotamuses, **27, 31**
humans' effects on animal and plant life, 10, 20
hyenas, **12**
iguanas, marine, 20
impalas, **8-9**

jaguars, 22, **23,** 26
lions, **5, 28**
lizards, 22
macaws, **21,** 22
Manu National Park, 22, **23,** 26, 30, 31. **31**
maps, **15, 29**
marabous, **29**
monkeys, 26
Mount Kenya, 28
natural selection, 18
Ngorongoro Crater, 28, 30, 31, **31**
okapis, 30
Olduvai Gorge, **13**
ostriches, 8
ozone layer, 4
Peru, 22
piranhas, 22
rain forests, 20-22, 26
rhinoceroses, **26-27**
savannahs, **5,** 12, 24, **24-25,** 26-30, **26-27**
sea lions, **19,** 20
Serengeti National Park, 30, 31
sloths, 26
South America, 12, 16-22, 26
turtles, Galapagos, 20
Virunga National Park, 28, 30, 31, **31**
volcanoes and volcanic formations, 16, 28, 30
water-holes and watercourses, **5,** 10, **11**
zebras, **5, 7,** 14, **15**

Titles in the World Heritage Series

The Land of the Pharaohs
The Chinese Empire
Ancient Greece
Prehistoric Rock Art
The Roman Empire
Mayan Civilization
Tropical Rain Forests of Central America
Inca Civilization
Prehistoric Stone Monuments
Romanesque Art and Architecture
Great Animal Refuges
Coral Reefs

Photo Credits

Front Cover: Alberto Larramendi-Juan Carlos Blanco/Incafo; p. 3: Gunter Ziesler; p. 5: A. Larramendi-J. C. Blanco/Incafo; p. 6: A. Larramendi-J. C. Blanco/Incafo; p. 7: Jose Luis Gonzalez Grande/Incafo y A. Larramendi-J. C. Blanco/Incafo; pp. 8-9: A. Larramendi-J. C. Blanco/Incafo; p. 11: A. Larramendi-J. C. Blanco/Incafo; p. 12: A. Larramendi-J. C. Blanco/Incafo; p. 13: A. Larramendi-J. C. Blanco/Incafo; p. 14: J. L. Gonzalez Grande/Incafo; p. 17: G. Ziesler; p. 19: D. Doubilet; p. 21: G. Ziesler; p. 23: L. McIntyre & G. Ziesler; pp. 24-25: A. Larramendi-J. C. Blanco/Incafo; p. 27: A. Larramendi-J. C. Blanco/Incafo & Joaquin Gomez Cano/Incafo; p. 28: A. Larramendi-J. C. Blanco/Incafo; p. 29: Luis Blas Aritio/Incafo & A. Larramendi-J. C. Blanco/Incafo; p. 31: L. Blas Aritio/Incafo, G. Ziesler, H. D. Dossenbach & A. Larramendi/Incafo; back cover: A. Larramendi-J. C. Blanco/Incafo.

Project Editor, Childrens Press: Ann Heinrichs
Original Text: Rafael Serra Naranjo
Subject Consultant: Susan Gray
Translator: Deborah Kent
Design: Alberto Caffaratto
Cartography: Modesto Arregui
Phototypesetting: Publishers Typesetters, Inc.

UNESCO's World Heritage

The United Nations Educational, Scientific, and Cultural Organization (UNESCO) was founded in 1946. Its purpose is to contribute to world peace by promoting cooperation among nations through education, science, and culture. UNESCO believes that such cooperation leads to universal respect for justice, for the rule of law, and for the basic human rights of all people.

UNESCO's many activities include, for example, combatting illiteracy, developing water resources, educating people on the environment, and promoting human rights.

In 1972, UNESCO established its World Heritage Convention. With members from over 100 nations, this international body works to protect cultural and natural wonders throughout the world. These include significant monuments, archaeological sites, geological formations, and natural landscapes. Such treasures, the Convention believes, are part of a World Heritage that belongs to all people. Thus, their preservation is important to us all.

Specialists on the World Heritage Committee have targeted over 300 sites for preservation. Through technical and financial aid, the international community restores, protects, and preserves these sites for future generations.

Volumes in the *World Heritage* series feature spectacular color photographs of various World Heritage sites and explain their historical, cultural, and scientific importance.